Real success is not to be sought after in the outer world but discovered in your inner world.... What matters is people. What lasts is love. What counts are true friends, and if you treasure these you can count yourself a success.

To Dad

You gave me the foundation for
a productive and successful life.
Thank you.

The

BASICS

of

SUCCESS

*...Keys to Achieving
Your Greatest*
Potential

Tim Connor

Blue Mountain Press ™

Boulder, Colorado

Library of Congress Card Number: 2005014114
ISBN: 0-88396-928-9

Certain trademarks are used under license.
BLUE MOUNTAIN PRESS is registered in U.S. Patent and Trademark Office.

Printed in the United States of America.
First Printing: 2005

This book is printed on recycled paper.

This book is printed on fine quality, laid embossed, 80 lb. paper. This paper has been specially produced to be acid free (neutral pH) and contains no groundwood or unbleached pulp. It conforms with all the requirements of the American National Standards Institute, Inc., so as to ensure that this book will last and be enjoyed by future generations.

Library of Congress Cataloging-in-Publication Data

Connor, Tim, 1942-
The basics of success : keys to achieving your greatest potential / Tim Connor. p. cm.
ISBN 0-88396-928-9 (trade paper : alk. paper) 1. Success—Psychological aspects. 2. Self-actualization (Psychology) I. Title.

BF637.S8C652 2005
158.1—dc22

2005014114

Blue Mountain Arts, Inc.

P.O. Box 4549, Boulder, Colorado 80306

Contents

INTRODUCTION

*D*o not be misled by the shortness of this book. Achieving success is not all that complicated, unless we choose to make it so.

For many, the benefits of success are elusive. These people struggle, search, and try year after year to create a life filled with financial security, nurturing relationships, and a sense of purpose and meaning.

Others appear to effortlessly achieve greatness, independence, and happiness as they travel through the days of their lives.

What is the difference between these two groups? Is it luck, a favorable early environment, good fortune, the right contacts, hard work, a powerful will to succeed, or some other measurable quality?

As a fellow traveler in search of success for over forty years, I do not claim to have an answer or the answer to your quest. I do not know the secrets, if there are any secrets, to success.

I have learned, however, that there are certain attitudes, actions, beliefs, and philosophies that when embraced and followed, ultimately lead to the higher ground.

In this book we will cover what I believe are the most common characteristics of successful people — regardless of age, sex, position, status, or whatever you would choose to define success.

I do not believe that success hinges on any single one of the qualities listed or those that I have chosen to leave out — which could easily have been included.

Success is not guaranteed to every human who walks the planet. However, the potential for success is bequeathed to each of us. It is not an accident or the result of believing that life owes you success.

Success is not: power, fame, wealth, prosperity, happiness, or independence. Once gained, there is no guarantee that the success you have achieved will be maintained in any recognizable or anticipated form. If success is lost, it is not destined to elude us forever.

Life offers no guarantees — just choices; no certainty — but consequences; no predictable outcomes — just the privilege of pursuit. People who succeed and fail come in all shapes, sizes, colors, ages, nationalities, and sexes. In the end, success is not what we achieve or accumulate, but who we become.

Life is not selective. It doesn't pick on some people while showering others with innumerable benefits or gifts. It is a perfect example of cause and effect in the ebb and flow of life. Life is not fair. It is not unfair, either. It just is.

In the end, people who want to succeed, do. Their success, however, may not resemble their early picture of what they thought their success should look like. People who fail want to fail. Oh, they may say they want success and its trappings, but in reality they do not believe in their hearts that they deserve it or will ever achieve it. We are all magnets. We attract into our experience that which is consistent with our inner beliefs, values, expectations, and desires.

Let's continue on your journey to greater success.

PRINCIPLE
NUMBER ONE:

PURPOSE

*I*n his classic bestseller *Think and Grow Rich*, Napoleon Hill discusses the importance of a "Definite Major Purpose" in life. It would be difficult for me to improve on his words that were written over forty years ago. I would like to give you my input on this vital concept and its relationship to motivation, success, and lifestyle.

Purpose, as defined by *Webster's* is: "the reason for which something exists, is done, made, etc. An intended or desired result, aim, or goal. To intend or resolve." Although I refer to my dictionary a great deal as a writer, I am more often than not confused by the use of certain words to describe other words. As I grow older, I am also finding the print is getting smaller and smaller (but that is my more recent problem). Dictionary definitions leave so much out regarding the essence of the word as a concept. Words are so much more than just words when you consider them more deeply. Let's take a few minutes and do that with "purpose."

Purpose is the determining factor in goals and objectives. If a person lacks a clear purpose in his or her life, career, or business, it is difficult to set and achieve meaningful goals. Without purpose, people easily lose their motivation or will to continue when life throws them a curve, pothole, or difficult challenge.

Without purpose it is difficult to develop any sense of satisfaction for accomplishments along life's path. And without purpose, people will change direction in life when the whim inspires them.

Purpose is similar to a personal mission statement. I will share mine with you to illustrate my points. My personal mission statement for over thirty years has been and is today "To learn as much as I can as I move through life and to share what I have learned with others who cross my path." This mission statement has become the foundation for my speaking goals, writing goals, and publishing efforts.

When I don't feel like writing, or would rather stay home than travel 10,000 miles to speak, or am not in the mood to write another book, my purpose — Life Mission — kicks in. The thought that often comes up is: either change your mission or purpose or get to it.

How are you doing today? Do you have a major purpose in life? Do you have a personal mission statement? Have you converted these into practical, rewarding, and meaningful goals and objectives? If not, what are you waiting for? Get to it.

The great pleasure in life is doing what people say you cannot do.

— *Walter Bagehot*

The Path

The path leads to nowhere and the path leads everywhere. As we travel, to each of us it soon becomes clear that no path is right or no path is wrong, but just is.

We are all where we are supposed to be, doing what we are supposed to be doing, and with whom we are supposed to be with.

There are no mistakes in the universe.

Others at times may appear to be lost, but judge not by appearances.

Life is not always what it seems.

Resist the need to guide or persuade your fellow travelers on the path. Your wisdom is like wind on the plains or snow falling on fresh snow. It fades into nothingness.

The messages we heed are all from within. All your words and
gentle counsel will be in vain.
The pace of our journey will vary from day to day and lifetime to
lifetime.
So trust the process of your life. Worry not about the
mountain, but focus on the terrain at hand.

Concern yourself only with your direction and not the endless road
ahead.

Your future can change in a heartbeat and the vision you held
of your ideal life
can be like the fading color of a summer sunset
or the exploding brightness of a wonderous sunrise.

It is not the pace, the direction, or the destination that should
fill your consciousness but only that you continue your journey
with confidence and peace
one step at a time.

PRINCIPLE NUMBER TWO:

COMMITMENT

*P*eople by the millions are bailing out of jobs, careers, businesses, relationships, and life in general. Many of these people lack commitment to a cause, lifestyle, purpose, or outcome. When it gets a little tough or uncomfortable, or they don't get the results they thought they would as quickly as they thought they should, their response is: "I'm outta here."

By commitment I am not suggesting you should endure an abusive relationship, continue to work for an organization that treats you unprofessionally, or hold on to a business that has been dead and buried. I am suggesting, however, that you consider your attitude about this concept. Is bailing out your knee-jerk reaction to difficult times, a failure, a stressful period in a relationship, continuous problems, or a bad year?

Many people today seem to lack any sense of real commitment and responsibility. Everyone wants to blame someone or something else for their problems or adversity. Difficult times can build strength and character, and can give you a real "high" when you overcome them. You cheat yourself out of this sense of accomplishment when things are easy.

Life is not meant to be easy, but living it is. The key to remember is that what is happening isn't really that important. There will always be "negative stuff" in your business, career, relationships, and life in general.

The secret is to understand that it isn't about what is happening "out there" in the world, but what is happening "inside" in your inner world of thought, feelings, and consciousness.

There is a tremendous benefit to sticking it out when life throws you curves. These times can be the most creative and motivating, and provide you with a tremendous opportunity for growth. Change in status in any business, career, or relationship brings both the need and benefit of new thinking and acting. Avoiding these times by quitting robs you of this joy of winning and learning.

How committed are you in all the areas of your life? Are you considering throwing in the towel? Have you experienced "more than you can handle" issues? Does it seem as if life is picking on you? Join the club, my friend. Everyone has issues, problems, or stuff in their life. It comes with the territory.

But you have a choice. You can look down and see the mud or look up and see the sun. You can give up, quit, and move on, or you can draw a line in the sand, saying: "This is where I make my stand." Just think of how many opportunities are missed because people quit one day, week, or month too soon.

Don't let it happen to you. Commit, go for it, never give up, and believe in your dreams, future, and life.

Be courageous... Have faith!
Go forward!

— *Thomas A. Edison*

PRINCIPLE NUMBER THREE:

PASSION

*K*eep your passion alive.

Passion is the great equalizer. It can make up for a lack of experience and knowledge. I am not suggesting that you not develop your knowledge or experience — only that until you do, your passion will be interpreted by others as a strong belief in yourself, your mission, and your purpose.

Passion is different from enthusiasm. The old, outworn cliché says: "Act enthusiastic and you will become enthusiastic." I have never subscribed to this philosophy. The reason is that if enthusiasm is an act that you use when things are going well, how do you behave when your life is falling apart? Are you just as enthusiastic about failure, more problems than you deserve, and any number of disappointments, frustrations, and adversities?

Passion is not an act. It is a way of believing. It is woven into your cellular structure just as much as your DNA. Passion — real passion for who you are and who you are becoming; where you are and where you are going; what you believe in, stand for, and would die for — shouts to the world: "I am here to stay; I am here to make a difference. I will leave my mark in this world. It may take my entire life, but I will not give up until my purpose and destiny are realized." Who do you know who is passionate about something? Anything? You can see it in their eyes, hear it in their voices, and sense it in their behavior.

How are you doing? Are you in love with where you are, where you are going, who you are becoming, and what you are contributing? Or are you living like more than eighty-five percent of the population with the attitude "same stuff, different day"? If you have lost or are losing your passion for life, your career, or a relationship, do whatever is necessary to get it back. Here are a few ideas to consider:

1. Count your blessings.

2. Accept the reality of how your life is unfolding.

3. Manage your expectations.

4. Let go of old garbage.

5. Accept yourself just as you are.

6. Live with an attitude of gratitude.

7. Find a way to serve your fellow humanity.

8. Do what you love, not what you must do.

Our greatest glory is not in never falling,
but in rising every time we fall.

— *Confucius*

PRINCIPLE NUMBER FOUR:
RESILIENCE

*O*ne of the critical skills for ongoing success is the ability to bounce back from adversity. Sooner or later in life everyone experiences failure, disappointment, setbacks, or the desire to keep on keeping on.

Over the years I have had my share of failures as well as successes. Failing doesn't make you a failure. Achieving success doesn't make you a success. Many people have hit bottom, only to climb out and achieve greatness, and many people have done great things only to end up broke, alone, and without any lasting feeling of accomplishment.

Success and failure are neutral concepts. What makes either of them positive or negative is not the event, circumstance, or situation but what is done with it along the path of life. No one that I have ever met has had a life filled with nothing but failure or success. Resilience is the ability to keep coming back, again and again and again. No matter how many times life throws you a curve or brings you to your knees, you try again. You try something new, something different, or something old in a new way. You refuse to give in or up. Here are a few ideas to consider when you feel like quitting:

1. It is temporary.

2. You need to learn a valuable lesson.

3. You need to be softened by life.

4. You need to give your life more integrity or character.

5. You need to learn to be an example for others.

6. You need to rid yourself of some arrogance or ignorance.

7. You need to grow in some area of your life.

8. You need to learn to laugh at yourself.

9. You need to learn to live in the present moment.

10. You need to learn to take life less seriously.

I am a testimony to resilience. If I can accomplish what I have in my career, having been brought to my knees again and again by failure, disappointment, and more problems than any one person should have — then you, too, regardless of your current station in life or circumstances, can rise again. All you have to do is reach inside and find the courage, strength, stamina, attitudes, self-belief, and self-confidence to rekindle your desire for what you believe you can do and will do.

Hang on to your dream, no matter how big it might seem to you. And don't let others convince you that you can't do it, won't do it, or shouldn't do it. Be true to yourself and your destiny. You have everything you need right now inside you to carry on. All you have to do is do it.

Know How to
Overcome Failure

"*F*ailure."
It's only a word.
But it carries with it so much pain
and so little concern,
so much frustration
and so little respect,
so much stress and so little
understanding
that people spend their lives
running through their days
in the hope of avoiding the long arm
of this little word.

To test your vision, you must risk
failure.

To temper your ego, you must attempt
the impossible.

To tell your story, you must
take a chance.

*To see beyond the horizon, you must
    spread your wings.*

*To be all you can be, you must
    stretch, flex, try, and go beyond
        your proven limits.*

*To bridge the silence, you must risk
    rejection.*

*To advance into the unknown, you must
    risk all your
            previous beliefs and emotions
        that feel so secure.*

*Failure is not negative. It is a teacher.
It molds, refines, and polishes you
        so that one day your light will
            shine for all to see.*

*It isn't the failure you experience
        that will determine your destiny,
    but your next step and then the next
        that will tell
            the story of your life.*

PRINCIPLE NUMBER FIVE:

FOCUS

*Y*ou tend to bring into your life that which is consistent with your focus. You can either focus on what is not working or what is; what you don't have or do; what you want or don't; what you believe in or don't. There is a great line (can't remember where I heard it, just know I am not taking credit for it) that says: "Be careful what you wish for; you might just get it."

One of my favorite quotes is by Arthur Ashe. He said, "True greatness is starting where you are, using what you have, and doing what you can."

Most winners in life are grateful for their blessings, and focus on what they want, have, and can do. By the same token, most losers focus on what is missing, where they are not, and what they can't do.

Let me give you an example:

Salesperson A complains constantly that prices are too high, brochures are not up to date, they don't have laptops or cellular phones, their territory is too small and has too few good prospects, there is inadequate internal support staff, it's raining. You get the picture: if they are doing poorly, they can find a reason why. (Other than themselves.)

Winners, on the other hand, learn to work with what they have. They improvise, innovate, adjust, compromise — whatever it takes to get the job done with the tools they have.

Let's look at one more quick example:

Manager A focuses on policies that are outdated, procedures that are no longer pertinent, and yesterday's issues or problems. Manager B understands a simple management truth: it is easier to apologize than it is to ask permission. Manager B focuses on getting the job done and the results, while Manager A focuses on the process.

I am not suggesting that some of these policies might not need to be changed. The key here is to do what you can within the framework of what is available to you, and get on with it. Whining about what is missing or can't be done keeps you stuck in the past. You have three options in any situation or circumstance: change it, accept it, or leave it.

A key characteristic in all leaders, winners, effective people, and productive and/or successful organizations is focus. What is your focus today? Is it on what you can or cannot do? Have or don't have?

To move the world, we must first move ourselves.

— Socrates

A Student in Life

There are so many opportunities to learn, to grow, and to
understand.
Life sends us a continual flow of teachers to guide and to
challenge
and to help and to correct. There are times
when I am ready to listen and so many times when I
haven't.

But the lessons are always present. Is it my stubbornness
or my ego, or is it my pride that stalls the learning?
If I could only get out of my own way,

I could learn when the time is right, the first time the lessons are
presented.
I could save myself so much pain.

The path of growth and understanding
is forgiving for a time. It is patient and loving for a time.
But time is running out. The pain of unlearned lessons haunts
me. The memories of
previous lessons not learned are etched on my soul.

They are repeated, louder now. But I still refuse to learn.
What will it take to master that
urge to resist? My reluctance to grow has a price. A price
that was low at first. But with each new opportunity to learn
the price went up. And in future days the price will
be higher still. I could reach the higher ground if I would let the
learning come. There, the rewards are sweeter.
The answer is simple:
be a student, able and loving. Love all the teachers
that life sends your way,
for life knows your needs, and resist as you will, life says, "I'll
be back another day."

PRINCIPLE NUMBER SIX:

GOALS

*E*ven a goal to do nothing is a goal. Everyone has goals; they just define them and move toward or away from them with a variety of perspectives or rationales.

I have set many goals that I have not yet reached. I have also had achievements in my life for which I never had a goal. I am sure you could say the same thing about your life. If this is true, what is the point of having goals in the first place?

There are two primary reasons for setting goals. First, they give you focus. Second, they give you direction.

Focus. Without focus, it is difficult to hit a bull's-eye, take a good picture, or avoid getting killed on a busy highway. Focus is an essential ingredient in successful people. They keep their eye on the ball. Yes, there are distractions, unexpected circumstances, and unknowns that will have an impact on you keeping your focus; but you must focus if you want to succeed.

Direction. The ultimate achievement of a goal is less important than the ability to continue working toward it. Many people achieve their goals and are disappointed once they get them. A goal once achieved is a milestone, yes, but you can't just sit back and rest on your success. Even a shark will die if it doesn't keep moving forward.

When a winner doesn't reach a goal, he or she reexamines what needs to change and then changes the time frame to achieve it. When a loser doesn't reach a goal, he or she reexamines and then changes the goal.

Don't worry about the destination; keep your eye on the ball in the present with what you can do now, not tomorrow. Do something every day to move a little closer to your objective.

You can't have everything in life that you want, but you can have anything. Keep the understanding of this principle clear in your mind.

Always bear in mind that your own resolution to succeed is more important than any one thing.

— Abraham Lincoln

PRINCIPLE NUMBER SEVEN:
CHOOSE WISELY

*E*very moment of our lives we make decisions. Some of these are life-changing, while others seem insignificant at the time. All choices lead to consequences. Some of these are positive, and some are negative. We always have options and choices. We may not like some of them, but we always have them.

The choices we are given present us with the opportunity to move steadily in the direction of a better way of life as we move toward our destiny. If we choose wisely, we move smoothly toward this destination. If we choose poorly, we are guided back to the correct path.

Each of us is responsible for the quality of our own life. To point the finger at anyone other than yourself for your life's outcomes is to live in frustration and denial. Each of us is free to choose any path. So choose wisely, for tomorrow's harvest is planted today.

It is interesting to note that people who are happy understand that they made the best choices they could at the time, given the information, experience, and insight that was available to them. When asked, "If you could live your life over, what would you do differently?" the response is almost always "Nothing."

Looking Back

I fight the pain of looking back on what could have been.
IF —
such a powerful word. If I could go back with the
knowledge of today.
I am here now, and those times have made me who I am.
But the unknowns
of tomorrow's possibilities still haunt me.
I missed so much, and I miss it still, and yet the yearning
to recapture those lost dreams has
lost its sting.
The tears of regret
still stain my heart. Will these feelings ever leave me, or are
they destined to be with me
always?
I can only look back now, no going back, no opportunity to
redo the errors of the past. And
are they errors or is it life as it was meant to be?
Answers I have few and questions
so many.
I can only look back with love and understanding and I
can only look ahead with patience and hope.
Tomorrow I will look back on today. My prayer is that
tomorrow's looking back will be done with
a smile.

PRINCIPLE NUMBER EIGHT:

CONVICTION

*Y*ou would be amazed at how many people quit just before they are about to achieve the success they have been working toward. They just get tired of waiting, trying, or dreaming, and give up. Why is this?

I believe it is for one of six reasons:

1. They really didn't want what they were going after in the first place.

2. They thought it would be easier.

3. They thought it would come sooner rather than later.

4. They lost belief in themselves or their mission or cause.

5. They let someone else discourage them or talk them out of wanting it.

6. They failed to realize that anything worthwhile takes time, faith, patience, and, yes, action.

Conviction is:

C Courage
O One day at a time
N No one can stop me
V Vision
I I can overcome
C Clarity
T Tenacity
I Inspiration
O Only you can do it
N Never quit

Is there an area in your life today where you are wavering? Thinking about giving up? I have been there. I know what it feels like to want to quit. But in the end I realized I didn't really want to quit; I just wanted to feel sorry for myself. Not a pretty picture.

No one can determine another person's limits of endurance or courage. No one can judge what another person is willing or not willing to do. Never let anyone talk you out of your dream, no matter how well-meaning they might appear.

Go for it. Keep at it. Just do it and enjoy the process. Don't expect that there will always be a crowd cheering you on. Much of success is enjoyed in quiet solitude, one moment at a time.

PRINCIPLE NUMBER NINE:

DETERMINATION

*W*hat does *determination* mean to you?

Is it sticking it out in tough times? Never quitting no matter what? Believing in yourself and your personal mission? Hanging in there regardless of the odds? Leaving the back door unlocked just in case?

I am always fascinated with textbook definitions. They so often only tell part of the story. Mr. Webster says determination is: "the quality of being resolute, firmness of purpose, the act of coming to a conclusion or resolving something, the settlement of a dispute." There is more, but the more I read, the more confused I become.

You can see that one word can have different meanings or interpretations. Just pick the definition you want. I believe there is much more to words than definitions.

Determination: You have it or you don't. You use it or you don't. It is either a part of your emotional makeup or it isn't. You believe in your destiny, mission, or purpose or you don't. You have faith in the fulfillment of your dreams or you don't. You work through issues, challenges, problems, failure, and adversity or you don't. You trust yourself to take the right actions and make the right decisions or you don't.

You believe in greatness, abundance, happiness, and success or you don't. You never settle for less, second best, or losing or you don't. You try one new strategy, approach, or action or you don't. You stay with something until it works, regardless of whether the outcome looks similar to your plan, or you don't. You try something new, original, or creative or you don't. You count your blessings or you don't. You are a survivor or you are not. You enjoy the process of learning, becoming, achieving, rather than just the outcome, or you don't.

How are you doing these days? Things a little tough right now? Or are you reaping the results of your previous determination? Either way, keep the vigil. You can't ever let up. Life won't let you. The moment you do, you invite life's scorn and wrath, and another opportunity for failure, disappointment, and pain.

Make Every Day an Adventure

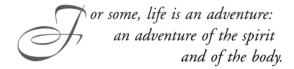or some, life is an adventure:
an adventure of the spirit
and of the body.

Each new day
begins with wonder and anticipation
for the newness that the day will offer.
It will bring opportunities for
growth,
love,
passion for being, and
the inner search for understanding.

Each day is unique, like a solitary snowflake
searching for itself and its place among the
millions of snowflakes that
have ventured on ahead of it.
Each new day adds color to the tapestry
of a well-lived life
and music to a carefree soul.

Each new experience blends to create a life
of purpose and passion
that shines like a lighthouse, sending its light
miles out to sea to guide weary or lost travelers
home to safety and the meaning
of their lives.

We are all here for a very short time.
The plan of this universe offers its share of
surprises and twists of destiny that curse the timid soul.
But those who live life as an adventure welcome
these turns in the road and quirks of fate.
For them, each day is packed full of as many sights and
sounds and tastes and emotions as they can experience.

For some, life is drudgery. It reeks of sameness
and routine, gray skies, dull sounds, bland people,
and suppressed emotions.

We make our days; they don't make us.
To live a life full of
adventure, learn to laugh more,
feel more,
share more,
learn more, and love more.

PRINCIPLE
NUMBER TEN:

MENTORS

*T*here is a wonderful way to cut twenty years off the learning curve in your career. It is to hang out with people who are where you want to be, or people who have done what you want to do. The key is to create a win-win relationship. A mentor is one of many ways to accomplish this objective.

What is a mentor? A mentor is a person who is interested in your success, happiness, well-being, and future, and wants to make a contribution. These people don't necessarily have to be in the same business, have the same interests, or have been successful in their chosen field. What a mentor brings to the mentor/mentee relationship is insight, feedback, integrity, a willingness to help, and genuine concern for the mentee.

The mentor always gains something from this relationship, but it's not always apparent what it is.

You don't need hundreds of mentors. One can accelerate your career; two can skyrocket it; and three can keep you learning and growing nonstop.

I suggest you look through your contacts and see if you can find someone who can contribute to your career success, and ask him or her to meet with you. If the person is a thousand miles away, call.

The key to a successful mentor/mentee relationship is setting the ground rules up front for each person's roles, expectations, agendas, time use, accountability, and feedback.

The right mentor can save you time, energy, and money. He or she can challenge your thinking, hold you accountable, help you reach your goals, and have fun in the process.

Find someone who can help you. Take advantage of his or her insight, experience, and knowledge.

PRINCIPLE NUMBER ELEVEN:
STRESS IS NORMAL

*S*tress in life is normal. Everything causes stress. There are positive things like promotions, marriage, relocation, starting a business, winning the lottery, retirement, having a baby, and any number of things that cause stress. There are also negative things such as failure, getting fired, getting divorced, missing a deadline, having a baby, getting promoted, starting a business, winning the lottery, the death of a loved one, relocating, etc., etc., etc.

Did you notice that I repeated some of the items in each list? Not a mistake, folks — it was intentional. Stress is not about what is happening, but how you respond to those things. (I just summarized my full-day seminar on managing stress in your life.)

Stressors are not positive or negative. A relocation can be positive for one person and negative for another. A promotion can do the same, and so can all of the others I mentioned, as well as all the ones I didn't. Wait a minute, Tim, how can the death of a loved one be interpreted as a positive stressor? Personally, I don't know of anyone who wishes for the death of a loved one. I am confident that somewhere out there in this world there is someone who will be relieved when a sick relative finally passes away, and that they no longer have to deal with the pain and humiliation that illness can bring.

Stress is not caused by events. If it were, everyone would have the same reaction or response to similar events, and we know that this isn't true. Stress can kill you or keep you alive. Stress can and will destroy your happiness if you do not learn to accept the reality of life and all of its issues, stuff, problems, and challenges.

Relax and enjoy the ride.

People's stress levels are at an all-time high. This is due to a number of factors:

1. The rapid pace of change and the amount of change.

2. The explosion of available information and the ease of acquiring it.

3. The drive toward better, more complete financial freedom.

4. The inner pressure felt by a large number of adults who still don't know what they are going to do when they "grow up."

5. More traffic, more and longer lines, more problems with products, services, and people, and fewer people to help.

6. The cost of goods and services that are spiraling upward at record speed.

These are just a few of the issues impacting the quality of life today. It is unfortunate, however, that many people let these put them in an early grave.

Everyone in this world has one thing in common — regardless of where he or she lives, age, profession, marital status, financial status, sex, color, religion, or nationality — and that is the desire to be happy. A recent survey I read said that seventy-five percent of the population needed to change something in their lives to be happier.

Change — where you live or work, to whom you are married, or whatever. One thing is for sure: you and I are not going to get out of this alive. So lighten up and relax. Enjoy the ride — it won't last forever, and the older you get, the faster the train seems to travel toward the final station.

You and I cannot stop the rapid pace of life and change around us, but we can slow ourselves down. We don't have to drop out, move to Vermont, and open a garden shop. We can learn to relax, slow down, control our pace, and generally enjoy the process and gift of life right where we are. It is simple, not easy, but simple. Here are a few things to consider.

1. Why are you in a rush; where are you trying to get to in such a hurry?

2. You can't do it all, see it all, have it all, learn it all, become it all, earn it all, read it all, etc., etc., etc., in one lifetime.

3. Happiness, success, peace of mind, fulfillment, or satisfaction is not an address, bank balance, age, position, weight, four-car garage, beauty, intelligent spouse, or kids. Happiness, success, peace, fulfillment, and satisfaction are not outside issues or circumstances, but inside attitudes and philosophies.

4. How much or how many will it take of something — or anything — for you to finally feel free of the need to continue at whatever pace you are traveling?

I am not suggesting we all become vegetables, waiting for life to pass us by. I am only recommending that you consider the trade-offs you are making in your health, relationships, and spiritual life.

PRINCIPLE NUMBER TWELVE:

IT'S ALL IN THE QUESTIONS

*O*ver the years, I have considered the difference between people who consistently do well in life — their careers and relationships — and people who struggle. One of the discoveries I have made is that the successful people have learned to ask the right questions of themselves and others. They have the courage to face the answers they get — even though they might be uncomfortable, cause personal unrest, or cause them to change a belief, habit pattern, or philosophy.

If you have not yet learned to ask yourself the right questions about:

- money
- life
- careers
- relationships
- life balance
- communication
- personal growth
- friendship

you may find yourself stuck in a position or way of life that is less than satisfying and/or filled with stress.

What do I mean by asking the right questions? Let me give you a brief example. Let's say you are struggling with a career decision. Here are a few sample questions you can ask. Note how each succeeding question probes deeper.

- Why am I unhappy in this career?
- What would I like to change?
- What is preventing those changes?
- Why am I afraid of the consequences of the new circumstances?
- What is it about the new circumstances that cause uncertainty?
- Why do I struggle with the issue of uncertainty?
- What do I need to feel secure?
- When will I know I have this security?
- Why is that so important?

Your questions will vary greatly depending on the subject. You can't develop a simple template that will work in your career as well as in a relationship. Spend the time developing AND asking the right questions, and you will be amazed at how quickly you can cut through all of the mental baggage that prevents your growth.

Now it is your turn. What area of your life needs some improvement? Why not develop a list of questions you can ask yourself to see where the trouble lies? Remember:

1. Don't force the answers.
2. Be willing to listen honestly.
3. Ask the questions while in a peaceful state of mind.
4. Be open and receptive to what you hear.
5. Keep asking deeper questions. Don't settle for a quick and easy solution.
6. Most of the causes of personal discomfort, stress, fear, and anxiety about life are inside-out propositions. Seldom does modifying your circumstances change who you are, what you believe, or your behavior.

SELF-FORGIVENESS

Self-forgiveness is one of the hardest things people can do for themselves. It is also one of the greatest gifts you can give yourself.

I don't believe that any of us is inherently bad — we just make dumb decisions or do foolish things. Many of us also believe that we won't get caught, and when we do, we feel guilty, silly, angry, stupid, or any number of other negative emotions. As a result, some of us carry these emotions around with us for weeks or even years. Why? Why do we feel the need to punish ourselves for lengths of time? We did what we did or believed what we believed at any given time in our lives either because of a lack of or a great deal of:

- experience
- knowledge
- understanding
- maturity
- faith
- self-belief
- self-acceptance
- personal growth
- time
- introspection
- self-evaluation

Looking back always gives us a clearer view of what we might have, could have, or should have done, thought, believed, and so on. Problem is, it's history.

The purpose of self-forgiveness is not to condone or let yourself off the hook for previous errors in judgment, misdeeds, poor behavior, or any number of issues that had negative consequences. Its ultimate purpose is to give you the opportunity to learn and grow from these past mistakes, failures, indiscretions, etc. and move on with dignity, confidence, faith, and belief. Problem is, if you can't forgive yourself, you may tend to take this lack of self-forgiveness into all of your future decisions, actions, relationships, activities, and behaviors.

What action, mistake, failure, transgression, etc. is lingering in your consciousness that, for whatever reason, you are unable to forgive yourself? One of the greatest acts of self-love is forgiving yourself and letting it — whatever it is — go. What is preventing you from forgiving yourself? Most people are far too hard on themselves when it comes to the realities of life's experiences.

Trust me, folks, I have made more mistakes in my life (and I know I am not finished making them) than any two people I have met in my life. I have chosen not to see them as mistakes but as lessons; not as failures, but as teachers; not as errors, but as life assignments. This works for me because it helps me keep all of my shortcomings, failures, and problems in perspective. I am not hiding from them or blocking them from my consciousness — just choosing to let them teach me whatever it is that I need to learn at any given period.

PRINCIPLE NUMBER FOURTEEN:
BOUNCE BACK

*E*veryone, at least once in their life, experiences some form of a setback, adversity, failure, or loss in at least one area of their life. Adversity can strike with or without notice. It can hit a relationship, a loved one, a career, a business, health, or financial status. No matter where or when it hits, the anxiety, stress, frustration, disappointment, fear, sadness, or panic leave the same feelings or emotions in its wake: a sense of hopelessness and/or despair.

Life is circular — not linear. First there is birth, then growth, then maturity, then death, followed again by birth or re-birth and so on. This is the law of the universe, whether it is life itself or a change in career or a relationship. I do not mean to imply that all relationships must die before their time, but they do eventually end. There is a big difference. Endings are different than death. Death is certainly an ending, but there are literally thousands of types of endings. Periods of life end — for example, youth. It is followed by adulthood. All careers end, if not by premature death, then by retirement or the beginning of a new or different career. Relationships end, if not physically, then a stage in the relationship — for example: lust, infatuation, or physical attraction is replaced by long-standing relationships with deep and abiding love.

Setbacks and adversity are often signals that some aspect of life has come to an end or needs to come to an end. They are wake-up calls, or what I call "choice points in life." Many people, myself included, on a number of occasions, resist endings from time to time. Sometimes, however, we embrace or encourage them. We want to continue life, business, or a way of life forever. Most people die with unfinished business left in them. It is seldom that there isn't something more that could have been said, done, seen, learned, or shared by someone who has passed on.

Life isn't fair, and it isn't unfair. It just is. Life is neutral. It brings each person unique opportunities to learn and grow as a result of the events or circumstances that cross his or her path. Everyone, I repeat, everyone, regardless of age, sex, nationality, religion, career status, or financial position is a student in life. Some people, upon an outward-in first glance, may "have it made." But do not judge by appearances only. Everyone has inner battles of one kind or another.

Adversity gives us the opportunity to do a number of things as we move through our lives. Some of them are: re-evaluate old life patterns that are not working; see ourselves more clearly as a contributor; develop new attitudes about life, relationships, money, people, work, etc.; observe how we handle the lessons we are given.

PRINCIPLE NUMBER FIFTEEN:
LIVE IN THE PRESENT

*L*ife is lived in the present, one moment at a time, not in the past or future. Our futures and memories are created in all of our NOW moments. Living in the present means staying focused on what is happening now, not what happened yesterday or may happen tomorrow.

People who focus on the past — mistakes, errors in judgment, hurtful words that were said in innocence, omissions, and disappointments — tend to bring a great deal of negative energy into the present.

People who focus on the future — expectations, desires, hopes, and "someday dreams" — tend to miss the value, joy, and wonder of their present moments.

Everyone has stuff. Neither you, nor anyone else, will ever be rid of it all. The key is to understand that you can't fix what happened yesterday and you can't fix anything tomorrow. You fix everything NOW.

Your soul wants for you what is your ultimate highest good. Your ego wants to look good, control, and protect itself. The ego tends not to like vulnerability and/or realness. This sets you up for hurt, pain, and rejection.

Learn to stay focused in the now. What you can do now. What you can say now. How you are feeling now. What you believe now. What you want to happen now.

Most people are rushing their way through life. They fail to take the time necessary to nurture their relationships, feed their mind, relax their body, or get in touch with their soul's desire for freedom and peace. Life moves relentlessly forward one day at a time, and there is nothing any of us can do to stop it or slow it down.

We are all getting older every day, but we don't have to grow older every day. Taking time to daydream, visit a friend, watch our children grow, or just play in our gardens is time well spent. There is a rush to tomorrow by all of us. We are being prodded into the future by faster computers, shorter delivery times, and a general need to have it, do it, and see it all: NOW!

Take time today for yourself. Take time to breathe in life, all of it: its color, splendor, smells, tastes, and sounds. From the smallest, most insignificant event to the things you have taken for granted.

Tomorrow will be here before you know it. Today will be a distant memory before you realize it. We create our futures and memories in the present. Go through life today, conscious of your surroundings. Why not take a long weekend walking through nature? There are a lot of lessons that nature can teach us, if we will only carefully observe and listen.

Today is a gift of life. Live it with gratitude and don't let the sun set today without seeing it, hearing it, and enjoying it.

Rushing to Tomorrow

 esterday is gone. Its hurts and its joys. Its successes and its mistakes and its frustrations and its desires.

Tomorrow is like a wisp of wind that comes and goes in an instant, teasing me with hope, unfulfilled aspirations and concern for a world I may never know.

Today, that's the miracle. Today is where my tomorrows are born and my yesterdays buried.

And now, this minute, is where life is lived one second at a time.

So why do we ignore each second as it passes as we
rush into the future, leaving behind so many feelings not felt,
   words not spoken, and love withheld?

What is this lure of tomorrow that is life's charade that draws
   us out of our now moments and into the ghost of our future?

Now is when I hug my child. Now is when I say I love you.
   And now I smell the aroma of life and nature's gifts.

None of these can be done tomorrow. And yet, if I wait, one day
   there will be no more tomorrows and I will have missed
                                                    all my todays.

PRINCIPLE NUMBER SIXTEEN:
SELF-ACCEPTANCE

*M*any people are searching for acceptance outside of themselves when they haven't yet learned to accept themselves. Self-acceptance is being okay with who you are, how you got there, and where you are going. It is having patience with yourself and loving yourself even when you make mistakes, fail, or do really stupid things.

Self-acceptance is a close relative of self-esteem. It is difficult to have one without the other, and if you have one, you will tend to have the other as well.

Why do people have low self-acceptance? There are many reasons, but most fall into the following categories:

1. The need to be perfect.

2. The need to be right.

3. The need for approval and to be liked.

4. Feeling inadequate due to some perceived lack of ability or skill.

5. Staying stuck in mistakes and errors in judgment in the past.

6. An extraordinary concern for other people's opinions and views about you.

7. A focus on imperfections rather than blessings.

8. A strong need to please others.

9. An ego that is out of control.

10. Emotional immaturity.

To accept yourself fully is to recognize that you will never be perfect. You are not finished making mistakes. You will fail again. Not everyone you meet will like you. A happy and contented life is not about what happens and why, but what you do with it or about it. People will disagree with you on numerous occasions. And, you will die with some unfinished business.

The key to gaining self-acceptance is to recognize that you are in process as a human being, and as a result of that process, your growth comes when you need it most. Your job is to take yourself lightly and what you do seriously. That doesn't mean walking around with a long face and sour disposition. It only means that you do the best you can with what you have at the time, and let go of the stuff that is not within your control — either emotionally, physically, or psychologically.

PRINCIPLE NUMBER SEVENTEEN:
MAINTAIN BALANCE

*O*ne of the issues facing many people today is the ability to maintain a sense of balance in their lives. My popular newsletter, *Life Balance*, is designed to help people who are faced with the increasing inability to maintain balance in their lives.

It is impossible to have total balance in your life. There are too many demands, issues, problems, needs, goals, and people to deal with. It is possible, however, to have enough balance to reduce the stress in your life while enjoying many of the gifts life has to offer.

There are several areas where we need to balance our lives. They are: family, work, financial, friends, social, spiritual, self-development, physical, personal interests, business or career interests, and fun.

At any given time, you can be way out of balance. For example, if you have just started a new business or career; if you have just had your first child; or if you are in a new relationship. During these times, you will most likely devote more time and energy to these activities while ignoring some of the others. The problem is if we stay out of balance in one area for a long period of time.

What are some steps we can take if we are out of balance?

1. Spend time deciding what is really important in your life, both short- and long-term.

2. Share your goals, dreams, needs, and frustrations about being out of balance with the people in your life who matter.

3. Learn to set better priorities.

4. Say "no" more often.

5. Determine where you are out of balance and ask yourself why.

6. Spend time better planning your days, weeks, months, and years.

7. Get up an hour earlier or go to bed an hour later.

8. Accept the fact that there are times in your life when you will be temporarily out of balance.

9. Simplify your life.

10. Simplify your life. (Not a typo... intended repetition.)

PRINCIPLE NUMBER EIGHTEEN:

SIMPLIFY

*E*verywhere you look, life is getting more and more complicated. While on the surface technology may appear to simplify your life, there are always trade-offs. What are some of the factors that seem to be moving our lives faster and making them more complicated? Here are a few:

- More traffic
- Increased consumer choices
- Faster computers and modems
- Cellular phones and pagers
- Time demands of all kinds
- The clock and calendar that seem to be moving faster and faster
- All kinds of personal and career stressors

I could go on, but you are well aware of the areas of your life that seem to push you to do more and faster.

I recently read a survey that said (I am always suspect of surveys, but here it is anyway): 70 percent of the U.S. population wanted more than anything else to simplify their lives — yet these very same people keep buying more and faster toys and stuff. Interesting paradox. We have been led to believe that more makes it easier. Faster makes it easier. I don't think so.

Here are a few things to consider:

1. Spend more time with nature. The relentless yet relaxing pace of nature can help you keep things in perspective.

2. Every week throw away or donate something, and don't replace it with something else.

3. Refuse to be prodded into buying the latest technology. Faster computer chips may bring you information faster, but I'll bet you can't handle the information you have access to now.

4. Take mini-retreats (an hour, day, weekend, or week) and get away to relax and reflect on what is really important in life.

5. Reduce the clutter in your life. Do you really need all that stuff?

6. Junk projects or activities that keep you stressed and filled with pressure and keep you from what is really important in your life.

7. Spend more time with the people in your life who really matter.

8. Don't let other people's agendas become yours.

9. Relax. You are not going to get out of this life alive — so what's the rush?

The Simple Things

*L*ife is so beautiful. It shows its splendor
in so many simple ways and with so many
simple things.

The sunset I
watch with awe, the laughter of a child. The ripples
on the water from a lonely duck

wash sleepily against the shore.
My daughter called today to say hello and the
waitress seemed glad to see me. A
friendly chat with my neighbor.
We are all on the same path together. Some of us see the
simple beauty and some of us miss it because of the chase.
It's the journey that counts, yet I have missed so many of the
simple things along the path.

The smile I missed,
the word not spoken, the hug withheld, the one I
longed for.

The joy that can never be, because
I missed the simple opportunity to see.
Regrets? I have a few. Did I cheat myself
by thinking that the simple things would always
be there?
They are now like a fading distant fog, masking their
image and hiding their sweet memory.
Today will be different. I will
inhale each moment and its beauty as if it were
my last.
Today
I will notice the simple things, for in an instant they will
be gone again.
I will notice and capture the simple things in my world
before it is too late.

PRINCIPLE NUMBER NINETEEN:

NO SELF-LIMITATIONS

*I*t has been said by many people smarter than I "that the only limitations we encounter in life are those self-limiting ones that we place on ourselves." If this is true, and at this point I am neither agreeing nor disagreeing with this premise, why then do so few people reach their full potential? Why do so many people feel stuck, out of control, and without hope in their lives?

Why do so many people give up, quit, settle, resign themselves to failure, or operate out of blame, anger, guilt, resentment, and self-pity when it comes to the quality of their lives? If this question were answered in a book with this title, it would never sell. Why? Because the very people we are talking about here do not want to take the responsibility for their lives. They insist on pointing their finger at something or someone else as the cause of their stations or circumstances in life.

I have been at the bottom of the barrel a few times in my life. I have also reached the mountaintop. I have met thousands of people in my travels as a speaker who believe they do not have any choices. They are stuck: in a job, business, relationship, way of life, neighborhood, climate, or career. You and I are not trees. We can change what we do not like. Why don't we? Fear, comfort, procrastination, wrong motives or reasons, and others' emotional manipulation of us and our acceptance of it.

The truth is, and I didn't just invent it or discover it, each of us came into this world headed for greatness in some way. We were engineered for success at birth and conditioned for failure along the way. We have forgotten our heritage. We have in our skulls the most magnificent organ ever created, a mind that can create whatever it chooses. There is nothing we cannot do. The skeptics out there are thinking, "Sure, Tim, I can fly."

I do not have the time or interest to deal with skeptics or critics. If that is their attitude, I will bet they take it into other areas of their lives as well. This is not about you or me flying, but realizing we can do whatever we put our minds to, as long as we put action into our dreams. Certainly there are some physical limitations in some areas or with some people. My major point here is that most of us could do more if only we would learn that most of our ceilings are self-imposed.

What inner mental images are you holding in your consciousness that may be holding you back? Is it the fear of failure or success? Is it the fear of rejection or public scorn? Is it an inner feeling of unworthiness? Or is it some other emotional issue or scar that you have failed to recognize or deal with?

Lord, grant that I might always desire
more than I can accomplish.

— *Michelangelo*

PRINCIPLE NUMBER TWENTY:
SUCCESS TRAITS

*S*everal months ago I began a survey on the traits of successful people. The response I received was overwhelming. The list below does not rank the items. That would have been impossible. As you will see, many of them could be number one. Please keep in mind that there may be others that are not on this list. This list is a compilation of my experience and the responses of over 1,000 successful people in all walks of life.

1. Live in the present.

2. Have meaningful personal and career goals and move toward them.

3. Invest in yourself. Have a regular, ongoing self-improvement program.

4. Manage your attitudes.

5. Have fun.

6. Live with passion.

7. Do what you love.

8. Communicate with integrity.

9. Work hard, sweat, make the effort.

10. Have self-discipline.

11. Have good personal health habits.

12. Have balance.

13. Have focus.

14. Be spiritually strong.

15. Have the ability to bounce back from adversity.

16. Have self-confidence.

17. Have ambition.

18. Have self-belief.

19. Have the ability to visualize success ahead of time.

20. Have commitment.

21. Take personal responsibility for your life.

22. Have a sense of humor.

23. Be optimistic.

24. Have positive self-esteem.

25. Keep reinventing yourself.

26. Have self-love and acceptance.

27. Have perseverance.

28. Have a personal vision for your life.

29. Be decisive.

30. Have strong desire.

31. Promote yourself.

32. Have gratitude.

Success

Everyone wants success, and yet we often don't know
when we have it.

For most, it is the maddening chase toward a better way of life
or more of something. More fame, power, recognition,
money, or stuff.
For some, it is the understanding of a loving partner, the love
a child, or the people that they can count on when life
throws them a curve.

I am coming to believe that success
is not more material wealth, but peace, happiness, contentment,
and love.

Most of all, love.

Real success is not to be sought after in the outer world but
discovered in your inner world. I am not condemning the stuff
of life. We all want the things that life offers. But we don't
need as much as we think we do.
Sooner or later you will discover as well that real success is to be
found in loving relationships. With your family, friends, strangers,
and anyone who crosses your path. It is a kindness
shared, support given and received, listening, giving, and caring.
These will endure while your car rusts, your toys break,
and you tire of the temporary gratifications that bring you
what you think is real.

What matters is people.
What lasts is love. What counts are true friends, and if you
treasure these you can count yourself a success. If you
lack these but abound in riches and their prizes
you will find an emptiness
that will never fulfill your needs or satisfy your desires.

PRINCIPLE NUMBER TWENTY-ONE:
HAVE FUN

*M*ost people take life far too seriously. You and I are not going to get out of this life alive, so why not enjoy the gift of life today as if the day were your last? One day you will be right. In my book *The Road to Happiness Is Full of Potholes*, I stress that one of the key traits of truly happy people is their ability to have fun.

Laughter is medicine for the soul. It helps you reduce the negative impact of the stressors in your life as well as see the problems you may be facing for what they really are: temporary teachers on the path of life.

What does having fun mean to you? When was the last time you played hooky and just spent the day doing what you wanted to do, not what you had to do?

I have a great many heroes. As I was recently considering their impact on my life, I realized that most of them made me laugh. There were Will Rogers, Mark Twain, George Burns, and Red Skelton. There were Groucho Marx and Steve Allen. How about Ernie Kovacs (for those of you old enough to remember him)? I could go on, but the point is: we all need to laugh more, smile more, and enjoy the gift of life more.

Few people will say on their deathbed that they should have worked harder, attended more meetings, made more money, or saved more money. Few people will say they should have learned more, taught more, become more, or seen more. I will bet that many, however, will say they should have laughed and smiled more.

Have some fun today. It doesn't matter how you define fun. Just have some. You will be better able to face the struggles, problems, challenges, and trials that life throws your way. While you are at it, why not brighten someone else's day as well? Do something to bring a smile to their face or help them have some fun. You both will feel better.

I just returned from a week-long speaking tour in Buenos Aires, Argentina. One thing I noticed about many of the people I met was how often they smiled and how happy they were. It was a wonderful trip and I can't wait to return. I like being around happy people.

Life always gets harder toward the summit —
the cold increases, responsibility increases.

— Nietzsche

To Be Free

*I*n each of us there is an urge to be free. To live life without worry and stress and distress and pain.

We all want to be free from

Frustration
  Guilt
    Resentment
      Blame
        Fear
          Anger
            Discouragement
              Worry

                Unfulfilled desires.

                To be really free
you must unlock the gate that holds your higher self imprisoned in darkness and anguish.

*The key to this gate
lies deep within your being. It is hidden behind years of
disappointment and unexpressed desires.
To find it you will have to look with courage and calm.*

*You must persist when you feel that the search is in vain.
For to be truly free the search must begin, and once begun, you
cannot go back.*

And it is not a search for timid souls.

*The road inside is cluttered with all sorts of baggage and illusions
as well as erroneous beliefs that have become etched on your
mind.*

Your key to freedom lies in your power to control your thoughts.

PRINCIPLE
NUMBER TWENTY-TWO:

RESOLVE

*T*hinking about quitting? A job? Career? Relationship? Project? Anything? Join the club. Sooner or later everyone thinks about quitting something. There is, however, a vast difference between quitting and wanting to quit. On the one hand you quit, and on the other you just want to think about it, but don't.

I have given up. I know the consequences of failure. I know how it feels to abandon a dream. I also know the thrill of overcoming and the benefits of resolve.

What is resolve? Is it persistence, commitment, dogged determination, or just plain old self-motivation? I don't have an answer to that, folks. I do know, however, that it costs more to fail than to keep on keeping on. There is a point in every relationship, career, project, or goal where our resolve to go on is tested.

Winners realize that they have to break through this barrier before they can enjoy the real fruits of their labor. Quitters, on the other hand, give up at the first sign of resistance or adversity.

Thinking about quitting something (a relationship, job, career, business, project, activity, way of life)? If you are, why not ask yourself a few thought-provoking questions.

1. Do you really want to quit?

2. What are your reasons for wanting to quit?

3. Are you willing to pay the consequences of quitting and starting over again?

4. What is so hard about your current situation or circumstances?

5. Is your pattern to quit before you get to enjoy real success?

6. What would you say to someone else who was in your position and said they were giving up?

7. Have you really done your best to make it work?

8. What will you lose by quitting?

9. How long have you been thinking about quitting?

10. Are you willing to put the energy, time, and resources into sticking to it?

11. What is the worst thing that could happen if you quit? The best?

12. What is the worst thing that could happen if you don't quit? The best thing?

Difficult questions, yes, but necessary to ponder prior to abandoning your goal, dream, or future.

PRINCIPLE NUMBER TWENTY-THREE:
PERSISTENCE

*I*t is unfortunate that many people quit just before they are about to have all their effort, patience, commitment, and belief pay off. Why is this? Why do people fail to stick with things? Well, for every person who has given up on something — anything — I will bet there are legitimate reasons.

I would like to share with you what I have discovered — some of the common reasons that cause people to fail to stick with things such as relationships, projects, careers, businesses, or simple activities and hobbies.

People lack persistence because they:

1. Are in too much of a hurry to get to the end of something.

2. Want it all now.

3. Feel they deserve it now.

4. Want to get it before someone else does.

5. Are afraid if they don't get it now, they never will.

6. Don't believe they have what it takes.

7. Lose confidence in themselves.

8. Lose confidence in their objective.

9. Don't really know what they want.

10. Are already there and they don't know it yet.

11. Think other people should give it to them.

12. Are afraid they might not be able to handle it if they do get it.

13. Are afraid of success.

14. Are afraid of failure.

15. Think it should be easier.

16. Feel it should come according to their personal timetable.

17. Hit roadblocks and stumble and don't get up again.

18. Believe what other negative people tell them about what they can and can't do.

19. Are great "starters" but poor "finishers."

20. Always have someone or something to blame.

21. Don't like lists. (This was just to see if you finished this one.)

A long list, I know, but I wanted to make sure I covered every possible reason. Any of them sound familiar to you?

PRINCIPLE
NUMBER TWENTY-FOUR:
EFFORT

We have heard it for years. Work smarter. Work more efficiently. Work more creatively.

You can work smarter and more effectively, but I don't believe there is any substitute for sweat, effort, and doing whatever it takes to achieve your goals, mission, and purpose in life. I believe in balance in life. I believe that there are other worthy elements in life besides work, careers, and running your business.

The key is to learn that if you hate your work, or you hate to work — unless you are independently wealthy or can live on $500 a year in a cabin in Vermont — you will live with a great deal of frustration, stress, anxiety, and disappointment. There are so many more reasons for working other than earning a living.

So learn to love your work. And if you can't love your current work, find work that you can learn to love. You will never be truly happy and successful doing what you hate. There is one exception to this rule, and that is knowing that what you may dislike in your work now is necessary so you can one day do what you love.

Work can:

1. Give your life a sense of meaning.

2. Give you self-satisfaction.

3. Give you a creative outlet for your talent.

4. Build your self-esteem.

5. Keep you from being bored.

6. Extend your range of influence.

7. Be your gift to society or the human purpose.

8. Broaden your contacts and the opportunity for friends.

9. Contribute to your personal development.

10. Add to your ability to converse with the people in your life.

11. Stretch your mind so that you don't atrophy with age.

12. Help you live longer.

PRINCIPLE NUMBER TWENTY-FIVE:
DO IT NOW

*P*rocrastination is a thief of time. It steals from the value and essence of your personal life and career. Why do people put things off? I could write a book on this, but I'll give it a try in twenty-five words or less.

They fear the future, overestimate their ability to get things done, don't know what to do or how to do it, thrive on pressure, set themselves up for failure, love disappointment, like being a victim, have too much on their plate, fail to set clear priorities, or have poor time-management or organizational skills.

What is the cost of procrastination?

1. Missed opportunities.

2. Increased stress.

3. Broken relationships.

4. Failure.

5. Increased anxiety and frustration.

6. The lack of respect for others.

That's enough, don't you think?

Develop a "Do-It-Now" philosophy.

Winners that I have observed in all walks of life tend to have several common traits. One that seems to stand out is the willingness and ability to Do It Now. How about you? Do you tend to put things off? To wait? To hope without taking action? To dream without commitment? To plan, but fail to take action? To scheme without substance? To brag without performance? To talk about what you are GOING to do, but never get started? A Do-It-Now philosophy says to the world:

- I believe in myself.
- I have faith in my endeavors.
- I know I can do it.
- I can overcome obstacles.
- If it is worth doing, it is worth doing now.
- I have confidence in my actions.

The social landscape is littered with people with good intentions. Good intentions mean squat without action. Good intentions are better than poor intentions, but are worthless without follow-through.

What are you putting off? A new exercise program? A planned self-development program? Telling someone close that you care, love them, or miss them? The price of failure is so much higher than the price of success. Don't wait another minute. Whatever it is, DO IT NOW.

You Can Make a Difference

*E*veryone can make a difference.

You can make a difference in the lives of your children by teaching them well.

You can make a difference in the world with all the other voices that echo your dreams and hopes for humanity.

We can all make a difference by holding fast to our values.

But most importantly, you can make a difference in your own life.

By choosing well, listening carefully, and acting decisively.

You can make a difference everywhere you look and with everyone you touch.

And making a difference is a role that's easy to fill and worthy of your effort.

Leaving behind lives that are better and richer and that are a witness to the fact that you lived and you loved.

What more is there?

Follow Your Heart

*T*here are two roads to follow in life,
and one is harder than the other.
There is the journey of
the mind or intellect —
and the journey of the heart.

Following your heart is filled with risk
and uncertainty,
and the road ahead is crowded with
souls trying but seldom succeeding
in their mission to love and serve.

There are times when the trip must begin
with a leap of faith — a leap that
seldom is secure.

There are times when the uncertain road ahead
fills our minds with fear that
we will never reach the other side.

But turn off your mind
and follow your heart.
It leads to softness, contentment,
and love,
though the way may not seem so at times.

If you would be free,
follow your heart.

Self-Assessment Questions

Please complete the following questions. Take your time, be honest, and give them adequate consideration. Use a separate sheet for your answers.

1. *Do you have a clear definition for success for your life?*

2. *Do you have clear, specific, written goals in all areas in your life?*

3. *Do you spend time each day in self-development?*

4. *Are you satisfied with your progress in life to date?*

5. *How would you like your life to be different?*

6. *Do you have a mentor, or do you belong to a mastermind group?*

7. *Are you moving steadily toward your goals?*

8. *If you could change anything about your life, what would you change?*

9. *Do you have a support system in place as you move toward your life's purpose?*

10. *Are you organized for success?*

11. *Do you use your time wisely to advance your life and career?*

12. *What is your response to failure, rejection, and adversity?*

13. *Are you in a career about which you can be passionate?*

14. *Have you ever given up, quit, or been so discouraged that you didn't know what to do next?*

15. *If you could change one thing about your job, what would it be?*

16. *Do you have a clear focus on your objectives and mission?*

17. *Do you regularly exert adequate effort to achieve the success you desire?*

18. *Do you have any self-limiting attitudes that impact your success?*

19. *Are you committed to your own personal success, and do you act consistently with that belief?*

20. *Do you make wise choices, taking into consideration their long-term impact?*

21. *Do you regularly work on your weaknesses?*

22. *Are you aware of all of your strengths?*

23. *Do you keep a journal of your successes, failures, etc.?*

24. *Are you having fun in your career or business?*

25. *Do you have a clear, definite purpose?*

About the Author

Tim Connor has been a full-time professional speaker and trainer since 1974. He has given more than 4,500 presentations in eighteen countries on sales, motivation management, supervision, and relationships. He is the author of thirty-six books, including the international bestseller *Soft Sell*. His self-help fiction books *The Ancient Scrolls* and *The Road to Happiness Is Full of Potholes* are also headed for bestseller status. Tim has been a member of the National Speakers Association since 1979 and earned his Certified Speaking Professional (CSP) designation in 1990.

Tim is also the founder of Master Speakers International, an elite group of seasoned, international speakers. To discuss a keynote address, custom seminar, ongoing in-house training program, or quantity discounts on his books and personal development products, please write or call Tim at:

Tim Connor, CSP
Connor Resource Group
P.O. Box 397
Davidson, NC 28036
Phone: 704-895-1230, Fax: 704-895-1231
tim@timconnor.com
www.timconnor.com